A Gift of
The Institute for the Study of
Human Knowledge

Sir
Richard Burton:

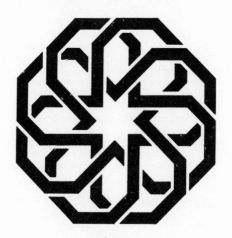

The
KASÎDAH
of Hâjî Abdû El-Yezdî

The
**OCTAGON
PRESS**
Ltd.

First impression in this Edition

Copyright © MCMLXXIV by The Octagon Press Ltd.

Requests for permission to reprint, reproduce, etc., to:
Permissions Department, The Octagon Press Ltd.,
14, Baker Street, London W1M 1DA, England

SBN: 900860 32 4

Printed and Bound in Great Britain by
Tonbridge Printers Ltd., Tonbridge, Kent

Sir Richard Burton

THE KASIDAH
OF
HAJI ABDU EL-YEZDI

CONTENTS

TO THE READER

THE Translator has ventured to entitle a "Lay of the Higher Law" the following composition, which aims at being in advance of its time; and he has not feared the danger of collision with such unpleasant forms as the "Higher Culture." The principles which justify the name are as follows:—

The Author asserts that Happiness and Misery are equally divided and distributed in the world.

He makes Self-cultivation, with due regard to others, the sole and sufficient object of human life.

He suggests that the affections, the sympathies, and the "divine gift of Pity" are man's highest enjoyments.

He advocates suspension of judgment, with a proper suspicion of "Facts, the idlest of superstitions."

Finally, although destructive to appearance, he is essentially reconstructive.

For other details concerning the Poem and the Poet, the curious reader is referred to the end of the volume.

F. B.

VIENNA, Nov. 1880.

THE
KASÎDAH

I

THE hour is nigh; the waning Queen
    walks forth to rule the later night;
Crown'd with the sparkle of a Star,
    and throned on orb of ashen light:

The Wolf-tail[1] sweeps the paling East
    to leave a deeper gloom behind,
And Dawn uprears her shining head,
    sighing with semblance of a wind:

The highlands catch yon Orient gleam,
    while purpling still the lowlands lie;
And pearly mists, the morning-pride,
    soar incense-like to greet the sky.

The horses neigh, the camels groan,
    the torches gleam, the cressets flare;
The town of canvas falls, and man
    with din and dint invadeth air:

---

[1] The False Dawn.

[9]

THE KASÎDAH

The Golden Gates swing right and left;
  up springs the Sun with flamy brow;
The dew-cloud melts in gush of light;
  brown Earth is bathed in morning-glow.

Slowly they wind athwart the wild,
  and while young Day his anthem swells,
Sad falls upon my yearning ear
  The tinkling of the camel-bells:

O'er fiery wastes and frozen wold,
  o'er horrid hill and gloomy glen,
The home of grisly beast and Ghoul[1],
  the haunts of wilder, grislier men;—

With the brief gladness of the Palms,
  that tower and sway o'er seething plain,
Fraught with the thoughts of rustling shade,
  and welling spring, and rushing rain;

With the short solace of the ridge,
  by gentle zephyrs played upon,
Whose breezy head and bosky side
  front seas of cooly celadon;—

---

[1] The Demon of the Desert.

THE KASÎDAH

'Tis theirs to pass with joy and hope,
  whose souls shall ever thrill and fill
Dreams of the Birthplace and the Tomb,—
  visions of Allah's Holy Hill.[1]

But we? Another shift of scene,
  another pang to rack the heart;
Why meet we on the bridge of Time
  to 'change one greeting and to part?

We meet to part; yet asks my sprite,
  Part we to meet? Ah! is it so?
Man's fancy-made Omniscience knows,
  who made Omniscience nought can
  know.

Why must we meet, why must we part,
  why must we bear this yoke of MUST,
Without our leave or askt or given,
  by tyrant Fate on victim thrust?

That Eve so gay, so bright, so glad,
  this Morn so dim, and sad, and grey;
Strange that life's Registrar should write
  this day a day, that day a day!

---

[1] Arafât, near Mecca.

Mine eyes, my brain, my heart, are sad,—
    sad is the very core of me;
All wearies, changes, passes, ends;
    alas! the Birthday's injury!

Friends of my youth, a last adieu!
    haply some day we meet again;
Yet ne'er the self-same men shall meet;
    the years shall make us other men:

The light of morn has grown to noon,
    has paled with eve, and now farewell!
Go, vanish from my Life as dies
    the tinkling of the camel's bell.

II

In these drear wastes of sea-born land,
    these wilds where none may dwell but
He,
What visionary Pasts revive,
    what process of the Years we see:

Gazing beyond the thin blue line
    that rims the far horizon-ring,
Our sadden'd sight why haunt these ghosts,
    whence do these spectral shadows spring?

What endless questions vex the thought,
    of Whence and Whither, When and
How ?
What fond and foolish strife to read
    the Scripture writ on human brow ;

As stand we percht on point of Time,
    betwixt the two Eternities,
Whose awful secrets gathering round
    with black profound oppress our eyes.

[13]

" This gloomy night, these grisly waves,
   these winds and whirlpools loud and
      dread:
What reck they of our wretched plight
   who Safety's shore so lightly tread ? "

Thus quoth the Bard of Love and Wine,[1]
   whose dream of Heaven ne'er could rise
Beyond the brimming Kausar-cup
   and Houris with the white-black eyes;

Ah me! my race of threescore years is short,
   but long enough to pall
My sense with joyless joys as these,
   with Love and Houris, Wine and all.

Another boasts he would divorce
   old barren Reason from his bed,
And wed the Vine-maid in her stead; —
   fools who believe a word he said![2]

And "' Dust thou art to dust returning,'
   ne'er was spoke of human soul"
The Soofi cries, 'tis well for him
   that hath such gift to ask its goal.

---

[1] Hâfiz of Shirâz.
[2] Omar-i-Kayyâm, the tent-maker poet of Persia.

"And this is all, for this we're born
    to weep a little and to die!"
So sings the shallow bard whose life
    still labours at the letter "I."

"Ear never heard, Eye never saw
    the bliss of those who enter in
My heavenly kingdom," Isâ said,
    who wailed our sorrows and our sin:

Too much of words or yet too few!
    What to thy Godhead easier than
One little glimpse of Paradise
    to ope the eyes and ears of man?

"I am the Truth! I am the Truth!"
    we hear the God-drunk gnostic cry
"The microcosm abides in ME;
    Eternal Allah's nought but I!"

Mansûr[1] was wise, but wiser they
    who smote him with the hurlèd stones;
And, though his blood a witness bore,
    no wisdom-might could mend his bones.

----

[1] A famous Mystic stoned for blasphemy.

THE KASÎDAH

"Eat, drink, and sport; the rest of life's
　　not worth a fillip," quoth the King;
Methinks the saying saith too much:
　　the swine would say the selfsame thing!

Two-footed beasts that browse through life,
　　by death to serve as soil design'd,
Bow prone to Earth whereof they be,
　　and there the proper pleasures find:

But you of finer, nobler, stuff,
　　ye, whom to Higher leads the High,
What binds your hearts in common bond
　　with creatures of the stall and sty?

"In certain hope of Life-to-come
　　I journey through this shifting scene"
The Zâhid [1] snarls and saunters down
　　his Vale of Tears with confi'dent mien.

Wiser than Amrân's Son [2] art thou,
　　who ken'st so well the world-to-be,
The Future when the Past is not,
　　the Present merest dreamery;

[1] The "Philister" of "respectable" belief.
[2] Moses in the Koran.

[16]

THE KASÎDAH

What know'st thou, man, of Life?
   and yet, forever twixt the womb, the
     grave,
Thou pratest of the Coming Life,
   of Heav'n and Hell thou fain must rave.

The world is old and thou art young;
   the world is large and thou art small;
Cease, atom of a moment's span,
   To hold thyself an All-in-All!

III

F<small>IE</small>, fie ! you visionary things,
   ye motes that dance in sunny glow,
Who base and build Eternities
   on briefest moment here below;

Who pass through Life liked cagèd birds,
   the captives of a despot will;
Still wond'ring How and When and Why,
   and Whence and Whither, wond'ring
   still;

Still wond'ring how the Marvel came
   because two coupling mammals chose
To slake the thirst of fleshly love,
   and thus the " Immortal Being " rose;

Wond'ring the Babe with staring eyes,
   perforce compel'd from night to day,
Gript in the giant grasp of Life
   like gale-born dust or wind-wrung spray;

Who comes imbecile to the world
    'mid double danger, groans, and tears;
The toy, the sport, the waif and stray
    of passions, error, wrath and fears;

Who knows not Whence he came nor Why,
    who kens not Whither bound and When,
Yet such is Allah's choicest gift,
    the blessing dreamt by foolish men;

Who step by step perforce returns
    to couthless youth, wan, white and cold,
Lisping again his broken words
    till all the tale be fully told:

Wond'ring the Babe with quenchèd orbs,
    an oldster bow'd by burthening years,
How 'scaped the skiff an hundred storms;
    how 'scaped the thread a thousand shears;

How coming to the Feast unbid,
    he found the gorgeous table spread
With the fair-seeming Sodom-fruit,
    with stones that bear the shape of bread:

[19]

THE KASÎDAH

How Life was nought but ray of sun
    that clove the darkness thick and blind,
The ravings of the reckless storm,
    the shrieking of the rav'ening wind;

How lovely visions 'guiled his sleep,
    aye fading with the break of morn,
Till every sweet became a sour,
    till every rose became a thorn;

Till dust and ashes met his eyes
    wherever turned their saddened gaze;
The wrecks of joys and hopes and loves,
    the rubbish of his wasted days;

How every high heroic Thought
    that longed to breathe empyrean air,
Failed of its feathers, fell to earth,
    and perisht of a sheer despair;

How, dower'd with heritage of brain,
    whose might has split the solar ray,
His rest is grossest coarsest earth,
    a crown of gold on brow of clay;

This House whose frame be flesh and bone,
    mortar'd with blood and faced with skin,
The home of sickness, dolours, age;
    unclean without, impure within:

Sans ray to cheer its inner gloom,
    the chambers haunted by the Ghost,
Darkness his name, a cold dumb Shade
    stronger than all the heav'nly host.

This tube, an enigmatic pipe,
    whose end was laid before begun,
That lengthens, broadens, shrinks and
    breaks;
    —puzzle, machine, automaton;

The first of Pots the Potter made
    by Chrysorrhoas' blue-green wave;[1]
Methinks I see him smile to see
    what guerdon to the world he gave!

How Life is dim, unreal, vain,
    like scenes that round the drunkard reel;
How "Being" meaneth not to be;
    to see and hear, smell, taste and feel.

---

[1] The Abana, River of Damascus.

A drop in Ocean's boundless tide,
   unfathom'd waste of agony;
Where millions live their horrid lives
   by making other millions die.

How with a heart that would through love
   to Universal Love aspire,
Man woos infernal chance to smite,
   as Min'arets draw the thunder-fire.

How Earth on Earth builds tow'er and wall,
   to crumble at a touch of Time;
How Earth on Earth from Shînar-plain
   the heights of Heaven fain would climb.

How short this Life, how long withal;
   how false its weal, how true its woes,
This fever-fit with paroxysms
   to mark its opening and its close.

Ah! gay the day with shine of sun,
   and bright the breeze, and blithe the
   throng
Met on the River-bank to play,
   when I was young, when I was young:

Such general joy could never fade;
   and yet the chilling whisper came
One face had paled, one form had failed;
   had fled the bank, had swum the stream;

Still revellers danced, and sang, and trod
   the hither bank of Time's deep tide,
Still one by one they left and fared
   to the far misty thither side;

And now the last hath slipt away
   yon drear death-desert to explore,
And now one Pilgrim worn and lorn
   still lingers on the lonely shore.

Yes, Life in youth-tide standeth still;
   in manhood streameth soft and slow;
See, as it nears the 'abysmal goal
   how fleet the waters flash and flow!

And Deaths are twain; the Deaths we see
   drop like the leaves in windy Fall;
But ours, our own, are ruined worlds,
   a globe collapst, last end of all.

[23]

We live our lives with rogues and fools,
 dead and alive, alive and dead,
We die 'twixt one who feels the pulse
 and one who frets and clouds the head.

And,—oh, the Pity!—hardly conned
 the lesson comes its fatal term;
Fate bids us bundle up our books,
 and bear them bod'ily to the worm:

Hardly we learn to wield the blade
 before the wrist grows stiff and old;
Hardly we learn to ply the pen
 ere Thought and Fancy faint with cold.

Hardly we find the path of love,
 to sink the self, forget the "I,"
When sad suspicion grips the heart,
 when Man, *the* Man begins to die:

Hardly we scale the wisdom-heights,
 and sight the Pisgah-scene around,
And breathe the breath of heav'enly air,
 and hear the Spheres' harmonious
 sound;

When swift the Camel-rider spans
   the howling waste, by Kismet sped,
And of his Magic Wand a wave
   hurries the quick to join the dead.[1]

How sore the burden, strange the strife;
   how full of splendour, wonder, fear;
Life, atom of that Infinite Space
   that stretcheth 'twixt the Here and
   There.

How Thought is imp'otent to divine
   the secret which the gods defend,
The Why of birth and life and death,
   that Isis-veil no hand may rend.

Eternal Morrows make our day;
   our *is* is aye *to be* till when
Night closes in; 'tis all a dream,
   and yet we die,—and then and THEN?

And still the Weaver plies his loom,
   whose warp and woof is wretched Man
Weaving th' unpattern'd dark design,
   so dark we doubt it owns a plan.

---

[1] Death in Arabia rides a Camel, not a pale horse.

[25]

Dost not, O Maker, blush to hear,
  amid the storm of tears and blood,
Man say Thy mercy made what is,
  and saw the made and said 'twas good?

The marvel is that man can smile
  dreaming his ghostly ghastly dream;—
Better the heedless atomy
  that buzzes in the morning beam!

O the dread pathos of our lives!
  how durst thou, Allah, thus to play
With Love, Affection, Friendship,
  all that shows the god in mortal clay.

But ah! what 'vaileth man to mourn;
  shall tears bring forth what smiles ne'er
  brought;
Shall brooding breed a thought of joy?
  Ah hush the sigh, forget the thought!

Silence thine immemorial quest,
  contain thy nature's vain complaint
None heeds, none cares for thee or thine;—
  like thee how many came and went?

THE KASÎDAH

Cease, Man, to mourn, to weep, to wail;
    enjoy thy shining hour of sun;
We dance along Death's icy brink,
    but is the dance less full of fun?

IV

WHAT Truths hath gleaned that Sage
    consumed
    by many a moon that waxt and waned?
What Prophet-strain be his to sing?
    What hath his old Experience gained?

There is no God, no man-made God;
    a bigger, stronger, crueller man;
Black phantom of our baby-fears,
    ere Thought, the life of Life, began.

Right quoth the Hindu Prince of old,[1]
    " An Ishwara for one I nill,
Th' almighty everlasting Good
    who cannot 'bate th' Eternal ill:"

"Your gods may be, what shows they are?"
    hear China's Perfect Sage declare;[2]
" And being, what to us be they
    who dwell so darkly and so far?"

---

[1] Buddha.
[2] Confucius.

[28]

" All matter hath a birth and death;
  'tis made, unmade and made anew;
" We choose to call the Maker ' God ' "—
  such is the Zâhid's owly view.

" You changeful finite Creatures strain "
  (rejoins the Drawer of the Wine)[1]
" The dizzy depths of Inf'inite Power
  to fathom with your foot of twine;"

" Poor idols of man's heart and head
  with the Divine Idea to blend;
" To preach as ' Nature's Common
  Course '
  what any hour may shift or end."

" How shall the Shown pretend to ken
  aught of the Showman or the Show?
" Why meanly bargain to believe,
  which only means thou ne'er canst
  know?

" How may the passing Now contain
  the standing Now—Eternity?—
" An endless *is* without a *was,*
  the *be* and never the *to-be?*

---

[1] The Soofi or Gnostic opposed to the Zâhid.

" Who made your Maker? If Self-made,
    why fare so far to fare the worse
" Sufficeth not a world of worlds,
    a self-made chain of universe?

" Grant an Idea, Primal Cause, the Caus-
    ing Cause,
    why crave for more?
" Why strive its depth and breadth to mete,
    to trace its work, its aid to 'implore?

" Unknown, Incomprehensible, whate'er
    you choose to call it, call;
" But leave it vague as airy space,
    dark in its darkness mystical.

" Your childish fears would seek a Sire,
    by the non-human God defin'd,
" What your five wits may wot ye weet;
    what *is* you please to dub 'design'd;'

" You bring down Heav'en to vulgar
    Earth;
    your maker like yourselves you make,
" You quake to own a reign of Law,
    you pray the Law its laws to break;

[30]

"You pray, but hath your thought e'er
    weighed
    how empty vain the prayer must be,
"That begs a boon already giv'en,
    or craves a change of law to see?

"Say, Man, deep learnèd in the Scheme
    that orders mysteries sublime,
"How came it this was Jesus, that
    was Judas from the birth of Time?

"How I the tiger, thou the lamb;
    again the Secret, prithee, show
"Who slew the slain, bowman or bolt
    or Fate that drave the man, the bow?

"Man worships self: his God is Man;
    the struggling of the mortal mind
"To form its model as 'twould be,
    the perfect of itself to find.

"The God became sage, priest and scribe
    where Nilus' serpent made the vale;
"A gloomy Brahm in glowing Ind,
    a neutral something cold and pale:

[31]

" Amid the high Chaldean hills
    a moulder of the heavenly spheres;
" On Guebre steppes the Timeless-God
    who governs by his dual peers:

" In Hebrew tents the Lord that led
    His leprous slaves to fight and jar;
" Yahveh,[1] Adon or Elohîm,
    the God that smites, the Man of War.

" The lovely Gods of lib'ertine Greece,
    those fair and frail humanities
" Whose homes o'erlook'd the Middle Sea,
    where all Earth's beauty cradled lies,

" Ne'er left its blessèd bounds, nor sought
    the barb'arous climes of barb'arous gods
" Where Odin of the dreary North
    o'er hog and sickly mead-cup nods:

" And when, at length, 'Great Pan is dead'
    uprose the loud and dol'orous cry
" A glamour wither'd on the ground,
    a splendour faded in the sky.

---

[1] Jehovah.

" Yea, Pan was dead, the Nazar'ene came
   and seized his seat beneath the sun,
" The votary of the Riddle-god,
   whose one is three and three is one;

" Whose sadd'ening creed of herited Sin
   spilt o'er the world its cold grey spell;
" In every vista showed a grave,
   and 'neath the grave the glare of Hell;

" Till all Life's Po'esy sinks to prose;
   romance to dull Real'ity fades;
" Earth's flush of gladness pales in gloom
   and God again to man degrades.

" Then the lank Arab foul with sweat,
   the drainer of the camel's dug,
" Gorged with his leek-green lizard's meat,
   clad in his filthy rag and rug,

" Bore his fierce Allah o'er his sands
   and broke, like lava-burst upon
" The realms where reigned pre-Adamite
   Kings,
   where rose the Grand Kayânian throne.[1]

---

[1] Kayâni — of the race of Cyrus; old Guebre heroes.

" Who now of ancient Kayomurs,
    of Zâl or Rustam cares to sing,
" Whelmed by the tempest of the tribes
    that called the Camel-driver King?

" Where are the crown of Kay Khusraw,
    the sceptre of Anûshirwân,
" The holy grail of high Jamshîd,
    Afrâsiyab's hall? — Canst tell me, man?

" Gone, gone, where I and thou must go,
    borne by the winnowing wings of Death,
" The Horror brooding over life,
    and nearer brought with every breath:

" Their fame hath filled the Seven Climes,
    they rose and reigned, they fought and
    fell,
" As swells and swoons across the wold
    the tinkling of the Camel's bell.

.   .   .   .   .

V

THERE is no Good, there is no Bad;
   these be the whims of mortal will:
What works me weal that call I " good,"
   what harms and hurts I hold as " ill: "

They change with place, they shift with
   race;
   and, in the veriest span of Time,
Each Vice has won a Virtue's crown;
   all Good was banned as Sin or Crime:

Like ravelled skeins they cross and twine,
   while this with that connects and blends;
And only Khizr[1] his eye shall see
   where one begins, where other ends:

What mortal shall consort with Khizr,
   when Musâ turned in fear to flee?
What man foresees the flow'er or fruit
   whom Fate compels to plant the tree?

---

[1] Supposed to be the Prophet Elijah.

For Man's Free-will immortal Law,
  Anagkê, Kismet, Des'tiny read
That was, that is, that aye shall be,
  Star, Fortune, Fate, Urd, Norn or Need.

"Man's nat'ural state is God's design;"
  such is the silly sage's theme;
"Man's primal Age was Age of Gold;"
  such is the Poet's waking dream:

Delusion, Ign'orance! Long ere Man
  drew upon Earth his earli'est breath
The world was one contin'uous scene
  of anguish, torture, prey and Death;

Where hideous Theria of the wild
  rended their fellows limb by limb;
Where horrid Saurians of the sea
  in waves of blood were wont to swim:

The "fair young Earth" was only fit
  to spawn her frightful monster-brood;
Now fiery hot, now icy frore,
  now reeking wet with steamy flood.

Yon glorious Sun, the greater light,
    the " Bridegroom " of the royal Lyre,
A flaming, boiling, bursting mine;
    a grim black orb of whirling fire:

That gentle Moon, the lesser light,
    the Lover's lamp, the Swain's delight,
A ruined world, a globe burnt out,
    a corpse upon the road of night.

What reckt he, say, of Good or Ill
    who in the hill-hole made his lair,
The blood-fed rav'ening Beast of prey,
    wilder than wildest wolf or bear?

How long in Man's pre-Ad'amite days
    to feed and swill, to sleep and breed,
Were the Brute-biped's only life,
    a perfect life sans Code or Creed?

His choicest garb a shaggy fell,
    his choicest tool a flake of stone;
His best of orn'aments tattoo'd skin
    and holes to hang his bits of bone;

Who fought for female as for food
    when Mays awoke to warm desire;
And such the Lust that grew to Love
    when Fancy lent a purer fire.

Where *then* " Th' Eternal nature-law
    by God engraved on human heart ? "
Behold his simiad sconce and own
    the Thing could play no higher part.

Yet, as long ages rolled, he learnt
    from Beaver, Ape and Ant to build
Shelter for sire and dam and brood,
    from blast and blaze that hurt and killed;

And last came Fire; when scrap of stone
    cast on the flame that lit his den,
Gave out the shining ore, and made
    the Lord of beasts a Lord of men.

The "moral sense," your Zâhid-phrase,
    is but the gift of latest years;
Conscience was born when man had shed
    his fur, his tail, his pointed ears.

What conscience has the murd'erous Moor,
    who slays his guest with felon blow,
Save sorrow he can slay no more,
    what prick of pen'itence can he know?

You cry the " Cruelty of Things "
    is myst'ery to your purblind eye,
Which fixed upon a point in space
    the general project passes by:

For see! the Mammoth went his ways,
    became a mem'ory and a name;
While the half-reasoner, with the hand[1]
    survives his rank and place to claim.

Earthquake and plague, storm, fight and fray,
    portents and curses man must deem
Since he regards his self alone,
    nor cares to trace the scope, the scheme;

The Quake that comes in eyelid's beat
    to ruin, level, 'gulf and kill,
Builds up a world for better use,
    to general Good bends special Ill:

---

[1] The Elephant.

THE KASÎDAH

The dreadest sound man's ear can hear,
    the war and rush of stormy Wind
Depures the stuff of human life,
    breeds health and strength for human-
    kind:

What call ye them or Goods or Ills,
    ill-goods, good-ills, a loss, a gain,
When realms arise and falls a roof;
    a world is won, a man is slain?

And thus the race of Being runs,
    till haply in the time to be
Earth shifts her pole and Mushtari[1]-men
    another falling star shall see:

Shall see it fall and fade from sight,
    whence come, where gone no Thought
    can tell,—
Drink of yon mirage-stream and chase
    the tinkling of the camel-bell!

.   .   .   .   .

----

[1] The Planet Jupiter.

VI

A<small>LL</small> Faith is false, all Faith is true:
    Truth is the shattered mirror strown
In myriad bits; while each believes
    his little bit the whole to own.

What is the Truth? was askt of yore.
    Reply all object Truth is one
As twain of halves aye makes a whole;
    the moral Truth for all is none.

Ye scantly-learned Zâhids learn
    from Aflatûn and Aristû,[1]
While Truth is real like your good:
    th' Untrue, like ill, is real too;

As palace mirror'd in the stream,
    as vapour mingled with the skies,
So weaves the brain of mortal man
    the tangled web of Truth and Lies.

---

[1] Plato and Aristotle.

What see we here? Forms, nothing more!
  Forms fill the brightest, strongest eye,
We know not substance; 'mid the shades
  shadows ourselves we live and die.

"Faith mountains move" I hear:
  I see the practice of the world unheed
The foolish vaunt, the blatant boast
  that serves our vanity to feed.

"Faith stands unmoved;" and why?
  Because man's silly fancies still remain,
And will remain till wiser man
  the day-dreams of his youth disdain.

"'Tis blessèd to believe;" you say:
  The saying may be true enow
And it can add to Life a light:—
  only remains to show us how.

E'en if I could I nould believe
  your tales and fables stale and trite,
Irksome as twice-sung tune that tires
  the dullèd ear of drowsy wight.

With God's foreknowledge man's free will!
  what monster-growth of human brain,
What pow'ers of light shall ever pierce
  this puzzle dense with words inane?

Vainly the heart on Providence calls,
  such aid to seek were hardly wise
For man must own the pitiless Law
  that sways the globe and sevenfold skies.

"Be ye Good Boys, go seek for Heav'en,
  come pay the priest that holds the key;"
So spake, and speaks, and aye shall speak
  the last to enter Heaven,—he.

Are these the words for men to hear?
  yet such the Church's general tongue,
The horseleech-cry so strong so high
  her heav'enward Psalms and Hymns
  among.

What? Faith a merit and a claim,
  when with the brain 'tis born and bred?
Go, fool, thy foolish way and dip
  in holy water buried dead!

[43]

THE KASÎDAH

Yet follow not th' unwisdom-path,
　cleave not to this and that disclaim;
Believe in all that man believes;
　here all and naught are both the same.

But is it so? How may we know?
　Haply this Fate, this Law may be
A word, a sound, a breath; at most
　the Zâhid's moonstruck theory.

Yes Truth may be, but 'tis not Here;
　mankind must seek and find it There,
But Where nor *I* nor *you* can tell,
　nor aught earth-mother ever bare.

Enough to think that Truth can be:
　come sit we where the roses glow,
Indeed he knows not how to know
　who knows not also how to 'unknow.

·　　·　　·　　·　　·

VII

Mᴀɴ hath no Soul, a state of things,
a no-thing still, a sound, a word
Which so begets substantial thing
that eye shall see what ear hath heard.

Where was his Soul the savage beast
which in primeval forests strayed,
What shape had it, what dwelling-place,
what part in nature's plan it played?

This Soul to ree a riddle made;
who wants the vain duality?
Is not myself enough for me?
what need of " I " within an " I " ?

Words, words that gender things !
The soul is a new-comer on the scene;
Sufficeth not the breath of Life
to work the matter-born machine?

THE KASÎDAH

We know the Gen'esis of the Soul;
    we trace the Soul to hour of birth;
We mark its growth as grew mankind
    to boast himself sole Lord of Earth:

The race of Be'ing from dawn of Life
    in an unbroken course was run;
What men are pleased to call their Souls
    was in the hog and dog begun:

Life is a ladder infinite-stepped,
    that hides its rungs from human eyes;
Planted its foot in chaos-gloom,
    its head soars high above the skies:

No break the chain of Being bears;
    all things began in unity;
And lie the links in regular line
    though haply none the sequence see.

The Ghost, embodied natural Dread
    of dreary death and foul decay,
Begat the Spirit, Soul and Shade
    with Hades' pale and wan array.

The Soul required a greater Soul,
    a Soul of Souls, to rule the host;
Hence spirit-powers and hierarchies,
    all gendered by the savage Ghost.

Not yours, ye Peoples of the Book,
    these fairy visions fair and fond,
Got by the gods of Khemi-land[1]
    and faring far the seas beyond!

" Th' immortal mind of mortal man! "
    we hear yon loud-lunged Zealot cry;
Whose mind but means his sum of thought,
    an essence of atomic " I. "

Thought is the work of brain and nerve,
    in small-skulled idiot poor and mean;
In sickness sick, in sleep asleep,
    and dead when Death lets drop the scene.

" Tush! " quoth the Zâhid, " well we ken
    the teaching of the school abhorr'd
" That maketh man automaton,
    mind a secretion, soul a word. "

---

[1] Egypt; Kam, Kem, Khem (hierogl.), in the Demotic Khemi.

" Of molecules and protoplasm
    you matter-mongers prompt to prate;
" Of jelly-speck development and apes
    that grew to man's estate."

Vain cavil! all that is hath come
    either by Mir'acle or by Law;—
Why waste on this your hate and fear,
    why waste on that your love and awe?

Why heap such hatred on a word,
    why " Prototype " to type assign,
Why upon matter spirit mass?
    Wants an appendix your design?

Is not the highest honour his
    who from the worst hath drawn the best;
May not your Maker make the world
    from matter, an it suit His hest?

Nay more, the sordider the stuff
    the cunninger the workman's hand:
Cease, then, your own Almighty Power
    to bind, to bound, to understand.

"Reason and Instinct!" How we love
  to play with words that please our pride;
Our noble race's mean descent
  by false forged titles seek to hide!

For "gift divine" I bid you read
  the better work of higher brain,
From Instinct diff'ering in degree
  as golden mine from leaden vein.

Reason is Life's sole arbiter,
  the magic Laby'rinth's single clue:
Worlds lie above, beyond its ken;
  what crosses it can ne'er be true.

"Fools rush where Angels fear to tread!"
  Angels and Fools have equal claim
To do what Nature bids them do,
  sans hope of praise, sans fear of blame!

.   .   .   .   .

VIII

THERE is no Heav'en, there is no Hell;
    these be the dreams of baby minds;
Tools of the wily Fetisheer,
    to 'fright the fools his cunning blinds.

Learn from the mighty Spi'rits of old
    to set thy foot on Heav'en and Hell;
In Life to find thy hell and heav'en
    as thou abuse or use it well.

So deemed the doughty Jew who dared
    by studied silence low to lay
Orcus and Hades, lands of shades,
    the gloomy night of human day.

Hard to the heart is final death:
    fain would an *Ens* not end in *Nil;*
Love made the senti'ment kindly good:
    the Priest perverted all to ill.

THE KASÎDAH

While Reason sternly bids us die,
    Love longs for life beyond the grave:
Our hearts, affections, hopes and fears
    for life-to-be shall ever crave.

Hence came the despot's darling dream,
    a Church to rule and sway the State;
Hence sprang the train of countless griefs
    in priestly sway and rule innate.

For future Life who dares reply?
    No witness at the bar have we;
Save what the brother Potsherd tells,—
    old tales and novel jugglery.

Who e'er return'd to teach the Truth,
    the things of Heaven and Hell to limn?
And all we hear is only fit
    for grandam-talk and nursery-hymn.

" Have mercy, man!" the Zâhid cries,
    " of our best visions rob us not!
" Mankind a future life must have
    to balance life's unequal lot."

[51]

" Nay," quoth the Magian, " 'tis not so;
    I draw my wine for one and all,
" A cup for this, a score for that,
    e'en as his measure's great or small:

" Who drinks one bowl hath scant delight;
    to poorest passion he was born;
" Who drains the score must e'er expect
    to rue the headache of the morn."

Safely he jogs along the way
    which 'Golden Mean' the sages call;
Who scales the brow of frowning Alp
    must face full many a slip and fall.

Here èxtremes meet, anointed Kings
    whose crownèd heads uneasy lie,
Whose cup of joy contains no more
    than tramps that on the dunghill die.

To fate-doomed Sinner born and bred
    for dangling from the gallows-tree;
To Saint who spends his holy days
    in rapt'urous hope his God to see;

To all that breathe our upper air
   the hands of Dest'iny ever deal,
In fixed and equal parts, their shares
   of joy and sorrow, woe and weal.

" How comes it, then, our span of days
   in hunting wealth and fame we spend
" Why strive we (and all humans strive)
   for vain and visionary end? "

Reply: mankind obeys a law
   that bids him labour, struggle, strain;
The Sage well knowing its unworth,
   the Fool a-dreaming foolish gain.

And who, 'mid e'en the Fools, but feels
   that half the joy is in the race
For wealth and fame and place, nor sighs
   when comes success to crown the chase?

Again: in Hind, Chîn, Franguestân
   that accident of birth befell,
Without our choice, our will, our voice:
   Faith is an accident as well.

THE KASÎDAH

What to the Hindu saith the Frank:
  " Denier of the Laws divine!
" However godly-good thy Life,
  Hell is the home for thee and thine."

" Go strain the draught before 'tis drunk,
  and learn that breathing every breath,
" With every step, with every gest,
  something of life thou do'est to death."

Replies the Hindu: " Wend thy way
  for foul and foolish Mlenchhas fit;
" Your Pariah-par'adise woo and win;
  at such dog-Heav'en I laugh and spit.

" Cannibals of the Holy Cow!
  who make your rav'ening maws the grave
" Of Things with self-same right to live;—
  what Fiend the filthy license gave?"

What to the Moslem cries the Frank?
  " A polygamic Theist thou!
" From an imposter-Prophet turn;
  Thy stubborn head to Jesus bow."

Rejoins the Moslem: " Allah's one
   tho' with four Moslemahs I wive,
" One-wife-men ye and (damnèd race!)
   you split your God to Three and Five."

The Buddhist to Confucius thus:
   " Like dogs ye live, like dogs ye die;
" Content ye rest with wretched earth;
   God, Judgment, Hell ye fain defy."

Retorts the Tartar: " Shall I lend
   mine only ready-money 'now,'
" For vain usurious 'Then' like thine,
   avaunt, a triple idiot Thou!"

" With this poor life, with this mean world
   I fain complete what in me lies;
" I strive to perfect this my me;
   my sole ambition's to be wise."

When doctors differ who decides
   amid the milliard-headed throng?
Who save the madman dares to cry:
   " 'Tis I am right, you all are wrong?"

"You all are right, you all are wrong,"
    we hear the careless Soofi say,
"For each believes his glimm'ering lamp
    to be the gorgeous light of day."

"*Thy* faith why false, *my* faith why true?
    'tis all the work of Thine and Mine,
"The fond and foolish love of self
    that makes the Mine excel the Thine."

Cease then to mumble rotten bones;
    and strive to clothe with flesh and blood
The skel'eton; and to shape a Form
    that all shall hail as fair and good.

"For gen'erous youth," an Arab saith,
    "Jahim's[1] the only genial state;
"Give us the fire but not the shame
    with the sad, sorry blest to mate."

And if your Heav'en and Hell be true,
    and Fate that forced me to be born
Force me to Heav'en or Hell—I go,
    and hold Fate's insolence in scorn.

---

[1] Jehannum, Gehenna, Hell.

[56]

THE KASÎDAH

I want not this, I want not that,
 already sick of Me and Thee;
And if we're both transform'd and changed,
 what then becomes of Thee and Me?

Enough to think such things may be:
 to say they are not or they are
Were folly: leave them all to Fate,
 nor wage on shadows useless war.

Do what thy manhood bids thee do,
 from none but self expect applause;
He noblest lives and noblest dies
 who makes and keeps his self-made laws.

All other Life is living Death,
 a world where none but Phantoms dwell,
A breath, a wind, a sound, a voice,
 a tinkling of the camel-bell.

. . . . .

IX

How then shall man so order life
  that when his tale of years is told,
Like sated guest he wend his way;
  how shall his even tenour hold?

Despite the Writ that stores the skull;
  despite the Table and the Pen;[1]
Maugre the Fate that plays us down,
  her board the world, her pieces men?

How when the light and glow of life
  wax dim in thickly gath'ering gloom,
Shall mortal scoff at sting of Death,
  shall scorn the victory of the Tomb?

One way, two paths, one end the grave.
  This runs athwart the flow'ery plain,
That breasts the bush, the steep, the crag,
  in sun and wind and snow and rain:

---

[1] Emblems of Kismet, or Destiny.

[58]

Who treads the first must look adown,
   must deem his life an all in all;
Must see no heights where man may rise,
   must sight no depths where man may fall.

Allah in Adam form must view;
   adore the Maker in the made.
Content to bask in Mâyâ's smile,[1]
   in joys of pain, in lights of shade.

He breaks the Law, he burns the Book,
   he sends the Moolah back to school;
Laughs at the beards of Saintly men;
   and dubs the prophet dolt and fool,

Embraces Cypress' taper-waist;
   cools feet on wavy breast of rill;
Smiles in the Nargis' love-lorn eyes,
   and 'joys the dance of Daffodil;

Melts in the saffron light of Dawn
   to hear the moaning of the Dove;
Delights in Sundown's purpling hues
   when Bulbul woos the Rose's love.

---

[1] Illusion.

Finds mirth and joy in Jamshid-bowl;
    toys with the Daughter of the vine;
And bids the beauteous cup-boy say,
    " Master I bring thee ruby wine!" [1]

Sips from the maiden's lips the dew;
    brushes the bloom from virgin brow:—
Such is his fleshly bliss that strives
    the Maker through the Made to know.

I've tried them all, I find them all
    so same and tame, so drear, so dry;
My gorge ariseth at the thought;
    I commune with myself and cry:—

Better the myriad toils and pains
    that make the man to manhood true,
This be the rule that guideth life;
    these be the laws for me and you:

With Ignor'ance wage eternal war,
    to know thy self forever strain,
Thine ignorance of thine ignorance
    is thy fiercest foe, thy deadliest bane;

---

[1] That all the senses, even the ear, may enjoy.

That blunts thy sense, and dulls thy taste;
 that deafs thine ears, and blinds thine
 eyes;
Creates the thing that never was,
 the Thing that ever is defies.

The finite Atom infinite
 that forms thy circle's centre-dot,
So full-sufficient for itself,
 for other selves existing not,

Finds the world mighty as 'tis small;
 yet must be fought the unequal fray;
A myriad giants here; and there
 a pinch of dust, a clod of clay.

Yes! maugre all thy dreams of peace
 still must the fight unfair be fought;
Where thou mayst learn the noblest lore,
 to know that all we know is nought.

True to thy Nature, to Thy self,
 Fame and Disfame nor hope nor fear:
Enough to thee the small still voice
 aye thund'ering in thine inner ear.

From self-approval seek applause:
    What ken not men thou kennest, thou!
Spurn ev'ry idol others raise:
    Before thine own Ideal bow:

Be thine own Deus: Make self free,
    liberal as the circling air:
Thy Thought to thee an Empire be;
    break every prison'ing lock and bar:

Do thou the Ought to self aye owed;
    here all the duties meet and blend,
In widest sense, withouten care
    of what began, for what shall end.

Thus, as thou view the Phantom-forms
    which in the misty Past were thine,
To be again the thing thou wast
    with honest pride thou may'st decline;

And, glancing down the range of years,
    fear not thy future self to see;
Resign'd to life, to death resign'd,
    as though the choice were nought to thee.

On Thought itself feed not thy thought;
   nor turn from Sun and Light to gaze,
At darkling cloisters paved with tombs,
   where rot the bones of bygone days:

"Eat not thy heart," the Sages said;
   "nor mourn the Past, the buried Past;"
Do what thou dost, be strong, be brave;
   and, like the Star, nor rest nor haste.

Pluck the old woman from thy breast:
   Be stout in woe, be stark in weal;
Do good for Good is good to do:
   Spurn bribe of Heav'en and threat of
   Hell.

To seek the True, to glad the heart,
   such is of life the HIGHER LAW,
Whose differ'ence is the Man's degree,
   the Man of gold, the Man of straw.

See not that something in Mankind
   that rouses hate or scorn or strife,
Better the worm of Izrâil[1] than Death
   that walks in form of life.

---

[1] The Angel of Death.

[63]

Survey thy kind as One whose wants
    in the great Human Whole unite;[1]
The Homo rising high from earth
    to seek the Heav'ens of Life-in-Light;

And hold Humanity one man,
    whose universal agony
Still strains and strives to gain the goal,
    where agonies shall cease to be.

Believe in all things; none believe;
    judge not nor warp by "Facts" the
    thought;
See clear, hear clear, tho' life may seem
    Mâyâ and Mirage, Dream and Naught.

Abjure the Why and seek the How:
    the God and gods enthroned on high,
Are silent all, are silent still;
    nor hear thy voice, nor deign reply.

The Now, that indivis'ible point
    which studs the length of inf'inite line
Whose ends are nowhere, is thine all,
    the puny all thou callest thine.

The "Great Man" of the Enochites and the Mormons.

Perchance the law some Giver hath:
    Let be! let be! what canst thou know?
A myriad races came and went;
    this Sphinx hath seen them come and go.

Haply the Law that rules the world
    allows to man the widest range;
And haply Fate's a Theist-word,
    subject to human chance and change.

This "I" may find a future Life,
    a nobler copy of our own,
Where every riddle shall be ree'd,
    where every knowledge shall be known;

Where 'twill be man's to see the whole
    of what on Earth he sees in part;
Where change shall ne'er surcharge the
    thought;
    nor hope defer'd shall hurt the heart.

But!—faded flow'er and fallen leaf
    no more shall deck the parent tree;
And man once dropt by Tree of Life
    what hope of other life has he?

THE KASÎDAH

The shatter'd bowl shall know repair;
    the riven lute shall sound once more;
But who shall mend the clay of man,
    the stolen breath to man restore?

The shiver'd clock again shall strike;
    the broken reed shall pipe again:
But we, we die, and death is one,
    the doom of brutes, the doom of men.

Then, if Nirwâna[1] round our life
    with nothingness, 'tis haply best;
Thy toils and troubles, want and woe
    at length have won their guerdon—Rest.

Cease, Abdû, cease! Thy song is sung,
    nor think the gain the singer's prize;
Till men hold Ignor'ance deadly sin,
    till man deserves his title "Wise:" [2]

In Days to come, Days slow to dawn,
    when Wisdom deigns to dwell with men,
These echoes of a voice long stilled
    haply shall wake responsive strain:

---

[1] Comparative annihilation.
[2] "Homo sapiens."

Wend now thy way with brow serene,
    fear not thy humble tale to tell:—
The whispers of the Desert-wind;
    the tinkling of the camel's bell.

שלם

THE KASÎDAH

NOTES

NOTE I

HÂJÎ ABDÛ, THE MAN

HÂJÎ ABDÛ has been known to me for more years than I care to record. A native, it is believed, of Darâbghird in the Yezd Province, he always preferred to style himself El-Hichmakâni, a facetious "lackab" or surname, meaning "Of No-hall, Nowhere." He had travelled far and wide with his eyes open; as appears by his "couplets." To a natural facility, a knack of language learning, he added a store of desultory various reading; scraps of Chinese and old Egyptian; of Hebrew and Syriac; of Sanskrit and Prakrit; of Slav, especially Lithuanian; of Latin and Greek, including Romaic; of Berber, the Nubian dialect, and of Zend and Akkadian, besides Persian, his mother-tongue, and Arabic, the classic of the schools. Nor was he ignorant of " the -ologies " and the triumphs of modern scientific discovery.

Briefly, his memory was well-stored; and he had every talent save that of using his talents.

But no one thought that he "woo'd the Muse," to speak in the style of the last century. Even his intimates were ignorant of the fact that he had a skeleton in his cupboard, his Kasîdah or distichs. He confided to me his secret when we last met in Western India — I am purposely vague in specifying the place. When so doing he held in hand the long and hoary honours of his chin with the points toward me, as if to say with the Island-King:

> There is a touch of Winter in my beard,
> A sign the Gods will guard me from imprudence.

And yet the piercing eye, clear as an onyx, seemed to protest against the plea of age. The MS. was in the vilest "Shikastah" or running-hand; and, as I carried it off, the writer declined to take the trouble of copying out his cacograph.

We, his old friends, had long addressed Hâjî Abdû by the sobriquet of *Nabbianâ* ("our Prophet"); and the reader will see

[72]

that the Pilgrim has, or believes he has, a message to deliver. He evidently aspires to preach a faith of his own; an Eastern Version of Humanitarianism blended with the sceptical or, as we now say, the scientific habit of mind. The religion, of which Fetishism, Hinduism and Heathendom; Judæism, Christianity and Islamism are mere fractions, may, methinks, be accepted by the Philosopher: it worships with single-minded devotion the Holy Cause of Truth, of Truth for its own sake, not for the goods it may bring; and this belief is equally acceptable to honest ignorance, and to the highest attainments in nature-study.

With Confucius, the Hâjî cultivates what Strauss has called the "stern common-sense of mankind"; while the reign of order is a paragraph of his "Higher Law." He traces from its rudest beginnings the all but absolute universality of some perception by man, called "Faith"; that *sensus Numinis* which, by inheritance or communication, is now universal except in those who force themselves to oppose it. And he evidently holds this general consent of mankind to be so

[73]

far divine that it primarily discovered for itself, if it did not create, a divinity. He does not cry with the Christ of Novalis, "Children, you have no father"; and perhaps he would join Renan in exclaiming, *Un monde sans Dieu est horrible!*

But he recognises the incompatibility of the Infinite with the Definite; of a Being who loves, who thinks, who hates; of an *Actus purus* who is called jealous, wrathful and revengeful, with an " Eternal that makes for righteousness." In the presence of the endless contradictions, which spring from the idea of a Personal Deity, with the Synthesis, the *Begriff* of Providence, our Agnostic takes refuge in the sentiment of an unknown and an unknowable. He objects to the countless variety of forms assumed by the perception of a *Causa Causans* (a misnomer), and to that intellectual adoption of general propositions, capable of distinct statement but incapable of proofs, which we term Belief.

He looks with impartial eye upon the endless variety of systems, maintained with equal confidence and self-sufficiency, by men of equal ability and honesty. He is weary

of wandering over the world, and of finding
every petty race wedded to its own opinions;
claiming the monopoly of Truth; holding all
others to be in error, and raising disputes
whose violence, acerbity and virulence are
in inverse ratio to the importance of the
disputed matter. A peculiarly active and
acute observation taught him that many
of these jarring families, especially those of
the same blood, are par in the intellectual
processes of perception and reflection; that
in the business of the visible working world
they are confessedly by no means superior
to one another; whereas in abstruse matters
of mere Faith, not admitting direct and
sensual evidence, one in a hundred will
claim to be right, and immodestly charge
the other ninety-nine with being wrong.

Thus he seeks to discover a system which
will prove them all right, and all wrong;
which will reconcile their differences; will
unite past creeds; will account for the present, and will anticipate the future with a
continuous and uninterrupted development;
this, too, by a process, not negative and
distinctive, but, on the contrary, intensely

positive and constructive. I am not called upon to sit in the seat of judgment; but I may say that it would be singular if the attempt succeeded. Such a system would be all-comprehensive, because not limited by space, time, or race; its principle would be extensive as Matter itself, and, consequently, eternal. Meanwhile he satisfies himself,— the main point.

Students of metaphysics have of late years defined the abuse of their science as "the morphology of common opinion." Contemporary investigators, they say, have been too much occupied with introspection; their labors have become merely physio-logico-biographical, and they have greatly neglected the study of averages. For, says La Rochefoucauld, *Il est plus aisé de connoître l'homme en général que de connoître un homme en particulier*; and on so wide a subject all views must be one sided.

But this is not the fashion of Easterns. They have still to treat great questions *ex analogiâ universi*, instead of *ex analogiâ hominis*. They must learn the basis of sociology, the philosophic conviction that mankind should be studied, not as a congeries of individuals, but as an organic whole. Hence the *Zeitgeist*, or historical evolution of the collective consciousness of the age, despises the obsolete opinion that Society, the State, is bound by the same moral duties as the simple citizen. Hence, too, it holds that the "spirit of man, being of equal and uniform substance, doth usually suppose and feign in nature a greater equality and uniformity than is in Truth."

Christianity and Islamism have been on their trial for the last eighteen and twelve centuries. They have been ardent in proselytizing, yet they embrace only one-tenth and one-twentieth of the human race. Hâjî Abdû would account for the tardy and unsatisfactory progress of what their votaries call "pure truths," by the innate imperfections of the same. Both propose a reward for mere belief, and a penalty for simple unbelief; rewards and punishments being, by the way, very disproportionate. Thus they reduce everything to the scale of a somewhat unrefined egotism; and their demoralizing effects become clearer to every progressive age.

[77]

Hâjî Abdû seeks Truth only, truth as far as man, in the present phase of his development, is able to comprehend it. He disdains to associate utility, like Bacon (Nov. Org. I. Aph. 124), the High Priest of the English Creed, *le gros bon sens*, with the *lumen siccum ac purum notionum verarum*. He seems to see the injury inflicted upon the sum of thought by the *à posteriori* superstition, the worship of "facts," and the deification of synthesis. Lastly, came the reckless way in which Locke "freed philosophy from the incubus of innate ideas." Like Luther and the leaders of the great French Revolution, he broke with the Past; and he threw overboard the whole cargo of human tradition. The result has been an immense movement of the mind which we love to call Progress, when it has often been retrograde; together with a mighty development of egotism resulting from the pampered sentiment of personality.

The Hâjî regrets the excessive importance attached to a possible future state: he looks upon this as a psychical stimulant, a day dream, whose revulsion and reaction disorder waking life. The condition may appear hum-

ble and prosaic to those exalted by the fumes
of Fancy, by a spiritual dram-drinking, which,
like the physical, is the pursuit of an ideal
happiness. But he is too wise to affirm or to
deny the existence of another world. For life
beyond the grave there is no consensus of
mankind, no Catholic opinion held *semper, et
ubique, et ab omnibus.* The intellectual faculties (perception and reflection) are mute upon
the subject: they bear no testimony to facts;
they show no proof. Even the instinctive
sense of our kind is here dumb. We may
believe what we are taught: we can know
nothing. He would, therefore, cultivate that
receptive mood which, marching under the
the shadow of mighty events, leads to the
highest of goals, — the development of Humanity. With him suspension of judgment
is a system.

Man has done much during the sixty-eight
centuries which represent his history. This
assumes the first Egyptian Empire, following
the pre-historic, to begin with B. C. 5000, and
to end with B. C. 3249. It was the Old, as
opposed to the Middle, the New, and the
Low: it contained the Dynasties from I. to

X., and it was the age of the Pyramids, at once simple, solid, and grand. When the praiser of the Past contends that modern civilization has improved in nothing upon Homer and Herodotus, he is apt to forget that every schoolboy is a miracle of learning compared with the Cave-man and the palæolithic race. And, as the Past has been, so shall the Future be.

The Pilgrim's view of life is that of the Soofi, with the usual dash of Buddhistic pessimism. The profound sorrow of existence, so often sung by the dreamy Eastern poet, has now passed into the practical European mind. Even the light Frenchman murmurs,—

Moi, moi, chaque jour courbant plus bas ma tête
  Je passe — et refroidi sous ce soleil joyeux,
Je m'en irai bientôt, au milieu de la fête,
  Sans que rien manque au monde immense et radieux.

But our Hâjî is not Nihilistic in the "no-nothing" sense of Hood's poem, or, as the American phrases it, "There is nothing new, nothing true, and it don't signify." His is a healthy wail over the shortness, and the miseries of life, because he finds all created things —

Measure the world, with "Me" immense.

He reminds us of St. Augustine (Med. c. 21). "Vita hæc, vita misera, vita caduca, vita incerta, vita laboriosa, vita immunda, vìta domina malorum, regina superborum, plena miseriis et erroribus . . . Quam humores tumidant, escæ inflant, jejunia macerant, joci dissolvunt, tristitiæ consumunt; sollicitudo coarctat, securitas hebetat, divitiæ inflant et jactant. Paupertas dejicit, juventus extollit, senectus incurvat, importunitas frangit, mæror deprimit. Et his malis omnibus mors furibunda succedit." But for *furibunda* the Pilgrim would perhaps read *benedicta*.

With Cardinal Newman, one of the glories of our age, Hâjî Abdû finds "the Light of the world nothing else than the Prophet's scroll, full of lamentations and mourning and woe." I cannot refrain from quoting all this fine passage, if it be only for the sake of its lame and shallow deduction. "To consider the world in its length and breadth, its various history and the many races of men, their starts, their fortunes, their mutual alienation, their conflicts, and then their ways, habits, governments, forms of worship; their enterprises, their aimless courses, their random achieve-

ments and acquirements, the impotent con-
clusion of long-standing facts, the tokens so
faint and broken of a superintending design,
the blind evolution (!) of what turn out to be
great powers or truths, the progress of things
as if from unreasoning elements, not towards
final causes; the greatness and littleness of
man, his far-reaching aims and short duration,
the curtain hung over his futurity, the disap-
pointments of life, the defeat of good, the success of evil, physical pain, mental anguish, the
prevalence and intensity of sin, the pervading
idolatries, the corruptions, the dreary hope-
less irreligion, that condition of the whole race
so fearfully yet exactly described in the Apostle's words, 'having no hope and without God
in the world' — *all this is a vision to dizzy and
appall, and inflicts upon the mind the sense of a
profound mystery which is absolutely without
human solution.*" Hence that admirable writer
postulates some "terrible original calamity;"
and thus the hateful doctrine, theologically
called "original sin," becomes to him almost
as certain as that "the world exists, and as the
existence of God." Similarly the "Schedule
of Doctrines" of the most liberal Christian

Church insists upon the human depravity,
and the "absolute need of the Holy Spirit's
agency in man's regeneration and sanctifica-
tion."

But what have we here? The "original calamity" was either caused by God or arose
without leave of God, in either case degrading
God to man. It is the old dilemma whose
horns are the irreconcilable attributes of good-
ness and omniscience in the supposed Creator
of sin and suffering. If the one quality be predicable, the other cannot be predicable of the
same subject. Far better and wiser is the essay-
ist's poetical explanation now apparently de-
spised because it was the fashionable doctrine
of the sage bard's day: —

> All nature is but art . . .
> All discord harmony not understood;
> All partial evil universal good. — (Essay 289-292.)

The Pilgrim holds with St. Augustine Absolute Evil is impossible because it is always rising up into good. He considers the theory of
a beneficent or maleficent deity a purely sentimental fancy, contradicted by human reason
and the aspect of the world. Evil is often the
active form of good; as F. W. Newman says,

" so likewise is Evil the revelation of Good."
With him all existences are equal: so long as
they possess the Hindu Agasa, Life-fluid or
vital force, it matters not they be, —

> Fungus or oak or worm or man.

War, he says, brings about countless individual miseries, but it forwards general progress
by raising the stronger upon the ruins of the
weaker races. Earthquakes and cyclones rav-
age small areas; but the former builds up
earth for man's habitation, and the latter ren-
ders the atmosphere fit for him to breathe.
Hence he echoes:

> — The universal Cause
> Acts not by partial but by general laws.

Ancillary to the churchman's immoral view
of "original sin" is the unscientific theory
that evil came into the world with Adam and
his seed. Let us ask what was the state of our
globe in the pre-Adamite days, when the tyrants of the Earth, the huge Saurians and other
monsters, lived in perpetual strife, in a destruc-
tiveness of which we have now only the fee-
blest examples? What is the actual state of the
world of waters, where the only object of life

is death, where the Law of murder is the Law of Development?

Some will charge the Hâjî with irreverence, and hold him a " lieutenant of Satan who sits in the chair of pestilence." But he is not intentionally irreverent. Like men of far higher strain, who deny divinely the divine, he speaks the things that others think and hide. With the author of "Supernatural Religion," he holds that we " gain infinitely more than we lose in abandoning belief in the reality of revelation"; and he looks forward to the day when "the old tyranny shall have been broken, and when the anarchy of transition shall have passed away." But he is an Eastern. When he repeats the Greek's "Remember not to believe," he means Strive to learn, to know, for right ideas lead to right actions. Among the couplets not translated for this eclogue is : —

> Of all the safest ways of Life the safest way is still to doubt,
> Men win the future world with Faith, the present world they win without.

This is the Spaniard's : —

> De las cosas mas seguras, mas seguro es duvidar ;

a typically modern sentiment of the Brazen

Age of Science following the Golden Age of
Sentiment. But the Pilgrim continues:—

> The sages say: I tell thee no ! with equal faith all
>   Faiths receive ;
> None more, none less, for Doubt is Death : they live
>   the most who most believe.

Here, again, is an oriental subtlety; a man who
believes in everything equally and generally
may be said to believe in nothing. It is not a
simple European view which makes honest
Doubt worth a dozen of the Creeds. And it is
in direct opposition to the noted writer who
holds that the man of simple faith is worth
ninety-nine of those who hold only to the ego-
tistic interests of their own individuality. This
dark saying means (if it mean anything), that
the so-called moral faculties of man, fancy and
ideality, must lord it over the perceptive and
reflective powers,—a simple absurdity! It produced a Turricremata, alias Torquemada, who,
shedding floods of honest tears, caused his vic-
tims to be burnt alive; and an Anchieta, the
Thaumaturgist of Brazil, who beheaded a converted heretic lest the latter by lapse from
grace lose his immortal soul.

But this vein of speculation, which bigots

brand as "Doubt, Denial, and Destruction;"
this earnest religious scepticism; this curious
inquiry, "Has the universal tradition any base
of fact?"; this craving after the secrets and
mysteries of the future, the unseen, the unknown, is common to all races and to every
age. Even amongst the Romans, whose model
man in Augustus' day was Horace, the philosophic, the epicurean, we find Propertius asking:—

> An ficta in miseras descendit fabula gentes
> Et timor haud ultra quam rogus esse potest?

To return: the Pilgrim's doctrines upon
the subject of conscience and repentance will
startle those who do not follow his train of
thought:—

> Never repent because thy will with will of Fate be
> not at one:
> Think, an thou please, before thou dost, but never
> rue the deed when done.

This again is his modified fatalism. He would
not accept the boisterous mode of cutting the
Gordian-knot proposed by the noble British
Philister—"we know we're free and there's
an end on it!" He prefers Lamarck's, "The
will is, in truth, never free." He believes man

to be a co-ordinate term of Nature's great pro-
gression; a result of the interaction of organ-
ism and environment, working through cos-
mic sections of time. He views the human
machine, the pipe of flesh, as depending upon
the physical theory of life. Every corporeal
fact and phenomenon which, like the tree,
grows from within or without, is a mere prod-
uct of organization; living bodies being subject to the natural law governing the lifeless
and the inorganic. Whilst the religionist as-
sures us that man is not a mere toy of fate,
but a free agent responsible to himself, with
work to do and duties to perform, the Hâjî,
with many modern schools, holds Mind to be
a word describing a special operation of matter; the faculties generally to be manifesta-
tions of movements in the central nervous
system; and every idea, even of the Deity, to
be a certain little pulsation of a certain little
mass of animal pap, — the brain. Thus he
would not object to relationship with a tailless
catarrhine anthropoid ape, descended from a
monad or a primal ascidian.

Hence he virtually says, "I came into the
world without having applied for or having

obtained permission; nay, more, without my leave being asked or given. Here I find myself hand-tied by conditions, and fettered by laws and circumstances, in making which my voice had no part. While in the womb I was an automaton; and death will find me a mere machine. Therefore not I, but the Law, or if, you please, the Lawgiver, is answerable for all my actions." Let me here observe that to the Western mind " Law" postulates a Lawgiver; not so to the Eastern, and especially to the Soofi, who holds these ideas to be human, unjustifiably extended to interpreting the nonhuman, which men call the Divine.

Further he would say, " I am an individual *(qui nil habet dividui)*, a circle touching and intersecting my neighbours at certain points, but nowhere corresponding, nowhere blending. Physically I am not identical in all points with other men. Morally I differ from them: in nothing do the approaches of knowledge, my five organs of sense (with their Shelleyan "interpretation"), exactly resemble those of any other being. *Ergo*, the effect of the world, of life, of natural objects, will not in my case be the same as with the beings most resembling me. Thus I claim the right of creating or modifying for my own and private use the system which most imports me; and if the reasonable leave be refused to me, I take it without leave.

"But my individuality, however all-sufficient for myself, is an infinitessimal point, an atom subject in all things to the Law of Storms called Life. I feel, I know that Fate *is*. But I cannot know what is or what is not fated to befall me. Therefore in the pursuit of perfection as an individual lies my highest, and indeed my only duty, the 'I' being duly blended with the 'We.' I object to be a 'selfless man,' which to me denotes an inverted moral sense. I am bound to take careful thought concerning the consequences of every word and deed. When, however, the Future has become the Past, it would be the merest vanity for me to grieve or to repent over that which was decreed by universal Law."

The usual objection is that of man's practice. It says, "This is well in theory; but how carry it out? For instance, why would you kill, or give over to be killed, the man compelled by Fate to kill your father?" Hâjî Adbû replies, "I do as others do, not because the murder was done by him, but because the murderer should not be allowed another chance of murdering. He is a tiger who has tasted blood and who should be shot. I am convinced that he was a tool in the hands of Fate, but that will not prevent my taking measures, whether predestined or not, in order to prevent his being similarly used again."

As with repentance so with conscience. Conscience may be a "fear which is the shadow of justice"; even as pity is the shadow of love. Though simply a geographical and chronological accident, which changes with every age of the world, it may deter men from seeking and securing the prize of successful villainy. But this incentive to beneficence must be applied to actions that will be done, not to deeds that have been done.

The Hâjî, moreover, carefully distinguishes between the working of fate under a personal God, and under the Reign of Law. In the former case the contradiction between the foreknowledge of a Creator, and the free-will of a Creature, is direct, palpable, absolute. We might as well talk of black-whiteness and

of white-blackness. A hundred generations
of divines have never been able to ree the riddle; a million will fail. The difficulty is in-
surmountable to the Theist whose Almighty is
perforce Omniscient, and as Omniscient, Pre-
scient. But it disappears when we convert the
Person into Law, or a settled order of events;
subject, moreover, to certain exceptions fixed
and immutable, but at present unknown to
man. The difference is essential as that between the penal code with its narrow forbid-
dal, and the broad commandment which is a
guide rather than a task-master.

Thus, too, the belief in fixed Law, versus
arbitrary will, modifies the Hâjî's opinions
concerning the pursuit of happiness. Mankind,
das rastlose Ursachenthier, is born to be on the
whole equally happy and miserable. The highest organisms, the fine porcelain of our family,
enjoy the most and suffer the most: they have
a capacity for rising to the empyrean of pleasure and for plunging deep into the swift-flow-
ing river of woe and pain. Thus Dante (Inf.
vi. 106):
                              — tua scienza

Che vuol, quanto la cosa è più perfetta
Più senta 'l bene, e cosi la doglienza.

So Buddhism declares that existence in itself implies effort, pain and sorrow; and, the higher the creature, the more it suffers. The common clay enjoys little and suffers little. Sum up the whole and distribute the mass: the result will be an average; and the beggar is, on the whole, happy as the prince. Why, then, asks the objector, does man ever strive and struggle to change, to rise; a struggle which involves the idea of improving his condition? The Hâjî answers, "Because such is the Law under which man is born: it may be fierce as famine, cruel as the grave, but man must obey it with blind obedience." He does not enter into the question whether life is worth living, whether man should elect to be born. Yet his Eastern pessimism, which contrasts so sharply with the optimism of the West, re-echoes the lines:

—a life,
With large results so little rife,
Though bearable seems hardly worth
This pomp of words, this pain of birth.

Life, whatever may be its consequence, is built upon a basis of sorrow. Literature, the voice of humanity, and the verdict of man-

kind proclaim that all existence is a state of
sadness. The "physicians of the Soul" would
save her melancholy from degenerating into
despair by doses of steadfast belief in the presence of God, in the assurance of Immortality,
and in visions of the final victory of good.
Were Hâjî Abdû a mere Theologist, he would
add that Sin, not the possibility of revolt, but
the revolt itself against conscience, is the pri-
mary form of evil, because it produces error,
moral and intellectual. This man, who omits
to read the Conscience-law, however it may
differ from the Society-law, is guilty of negli-
gence. That man, who obscures the light of
Nature with sophistries, becomes incapable of
discerning his own truths. In both cases error,
deliberately adopted, is succeeded by suffering
which, we are told, comes in justice and benevolence as a warning, a remedy, and a chas-
tisement.

But the Pilgrim is dissatisfied with the idea
that evil originates in the individual actions of
free agents, ourselves and others. This doctrine fails to account for its characteristics,—
essentiality and universality. That creatures
endowed with the mere possibility of liberty

should not always choose the Good appears natural. But that of the milliards of human beings who have inhabited the Earth, not one should have been found invariably to choose Good, proves how insufficient is the solution. Hence no one believes in the existence of the complete man under the present state of things. The Hâjî rejects all popular and mythical explanation by the Fall of "Adam," the innate depravity of human nature, and the absolute perfection of certain Incarnations, which argues their divinity. He can only wail over the prevalence of evil, assume its foundation to be error, and purpose to abate it by unrooting that Ignorance which bears and feeds it.

His "eschatology," like that of the Soofis generally, is vague and shadowy. He may lean towards the doctrine of Marc Aurelius, "The unripe grape, the ripe and the dried: all things are changes not into nothing, but into that which is not at present." This is one of the *monstruosa opinionum portenta* mentioned by the XIXth General Council, alias the First Council of the Vatican. But he only accepts it with a limitation. He cleaves to the ethical, not to the intellectual, worship of "Nature," which moderns define to be an "unscientific and imaginary synonym for the sum total of observed phenomena." Consequently he holds to the "dark and degrading doctrines of the Materialist," the "Hylotheist"; in opposition to the spiritualist, a distinction far more marked in the West than in the East. Europe draws a hard, dry line between Spirit and Matter: Asia does not.

Among us the Idealist objects to the Materialists that the latter cannot agree upon fundamental points; that they cannot define what is an atom; that they cannot account for the transformation of physical action and molecular motion into consciousness; and *vice versâ*, that they cannot say what matter is; and, lastly, that Berkeley and his school have proved the existence of spirit while denying that of matter.

The Materialists reply that the want of agreement shows only a study insufficiently advanced; that man cannot describe an atom, because he is still an infant in science, yet there is no reason why his mature manhood should not pass through error and incapacity to truth and knowledge; that consciousness becomes a property of matter when certain conditions are present; that Hyle (ὕλη) or Matter may be provisionally defined as "phenomena with a substructure of their own, transcendental and eternal, subject to the action, direct or indirect, of the five senses, whilst its properties present themselves in three states, the solid, the liquid, and the gaseous." To casuistical Berkeley they prefer the common sense of mankind. They ask the idealist and the spiritualist why they cannot find names for themselves without borrowing from a "dark and degraded" school; why the former must call himself after his eye *(idein)*; the latter after his breath *(spiritus)?* Thus the Hâjî twits them with affixing their own limitations to their own Almighty Power, and, as Socrates said, with bringing down Heaven to the market-place.

Modern thought tends more and more to reject crude idealism and to support the monistic theory, the double aspect, the transfigured realism. It discusses the Nature of Things in Themselves. To the question, is there anything outside of us which corresponds with our sensations? that is to say, is the whole world

simply "I," they reply that obviously there is
a something else; and that this something else
produces the brain-disturbance which is called
sensation. Instinct orders us to do something;
Reason (the balance of faculties) directs; and
the strongest motive controls. Modern Science, by the discovery of Radiant Matter, a
fourth condition, seems to conciliate the two
schools. " La découverte d'un quatrième état
de la matière," says a Reviewer, " c'est la
porte ouverte à l'infini de ses transformations;
c'est l'homme invisible et impalpable de même
possible sans cesser d'être substantiel; c'est
le monde des esprits entrant sans absurdité
dans la domaine des hypothèses scientifiques;
c'est la possibilité pour le matérialiste de croire
à la vie d'outre tombe, sans renoncer au substratum matériel qu'il croit nécessaire au maintien de l'individualité."

With Hâjî Abdû the soul is not material,
for that would be a contradiction of terms. He
regards it, with many moderns, as a state of
things, not a thing; a convenient word denoting the sense of personality, of individual identity. In its ghostly signification he discovers an
artificial dogma which could hardly belong to

the brutal savages of the Stone Age. He finds
it in the funereal books of ancient Egypt,
whence probably it passed to the Zendavesta
and the Vedas. In the Hebrew Pentateuch, of
which part is still attributed to Moses, it is unknown, or, rather, it is deliberately ignored by
the author or authors. The early Christians
could not agree upon the subject; Origen ad-
vocated the pre-existence of men's souls, sup-
posing them to have been all created at one
time and successively embodied. Others make
Spirit born with the hour of birth: and so forth.

But the brain-action or, if you so phrase it,
the mind, is not confined to the reasoning faculties; nor can we afford to ignore the sentiments, the affections which are, perhaps, the
most potent realities of life. Their loud af-
firmative voice contrasts strongly with the
titubant accents of the intellect. They seem to
demand a future life, even a state of rewards
and punishments from the Maker of the world,
the *Ortolano Eterno*,[1] the Potter of the East,

---

[1] The Eternal Gardener : so the old inscription
saying : —

$$\text{Homo} \begin{cases} \text{locatus est in} \\ \text{damnatus est in} \\ \text{humatus est in} \\ \text{renatus est in} \end{cases} \text{horto}$$

[99]

the Watchmaker of the West. They protest against the idea of annihilation. They revolt at the notion of eternal parting from parents, kinsmen and friends. Yet the dogma of a future life is by no means catholic and universal. The Anglo-European race apparently cannot exist without it, and we have lately heard of the "Aryan Soul-land." On the other hand many of the Buddhist and even the Brahman Schools preach Nirwâna (comparative non-existence) and Parinirwâna (absolute nothingness). Moreover, the great Turanian family, actually occupying all Eastern Asia, has ever ignored it; and the 200,000,000 of Chinese Confucians, the mass of the nation, protest emphatically against the mainstay of the western creeds, because it "unfits men for the business and duty of life by fixing their speculations on an unknown world." And even its votaries, in all ages, races and faiths, cannot deny that the next world is a copy, more or less idealized, of the present; and that it lacks a single particular savouring of originality. It is in fact a mere continuation; and the continuation is "not proven."

It is most hard to be a man ;

and the Pilgrim's sole consolation is in self-cultivation, and in the pleasures of the affections. This sympathy may be an indirect self-love, a reflection of the light of egotism: still it is so transferred as to imply a different system of convictions. It requires a different name: to call benevolence "self-love" is to make the fruit or flower not only depend upon a root for development (which is true), but the very root itself (which is false). And, finally, his ideal is of the highest: his praise is reserved for:

> — Lives
> Lived in obedience to the inner law
> Which cannot alter.

NOTE II

A FEW words concerning the Kasîdah itself. Our Hâjî begins with a *mise-en-scène*; and takes leave of the Caravan setting out for Mecca. He sees the " Wolf's tail " *(Dum-i-gurg)*, the λυκαυγές, or wolf-gleam, the Diluculum, the Zodiacal dawn-light, the first faint brushes of white radiating from below the Eastern horizon. It is accompanied by the morning-breath *(Dam-i-Subh)*, the current of air, almost imperceptible except by the increase of cold, which Moslem physiologists suppose to be the early prayer offered by Nature to the First Cause. The Ghoul-i-Biyâbân (Desert-Demon) is evidently the personification of man's fears and of the dangers that surround travelling in the wilds. The " wold-where-none-save-He (Allah)-can-dwell " is a great and terrible wilderness *(Dasht-i-lâ-siwâ Hu)*; and Allah's Holy Hill is Arafât, near Mecca, which the Caravan reaches after

passing through Medina. The first section
ends with a sore lament that the "meetings of
this world take place upon the highway of
Separation;" and the original also has:—

The chill of sorrow numbs my thought: methinks I
hear the passing knell;
As dies across yon thin blue line the tinkling of the
Camel-bell.

The next section quotes the various aspects
under which Life appeared to the wise and
foolish teachers of humanity. First comes
Hafiz, whose well-known lines are quoted beginning with Shab-i-târîk o bîm-i-mauj, etc.
Hûr is the plural of Ahwar, in full Ahwar
el-Ayn, a maid whose eyes are intensely white
where they should be white, and black elsewhere: hence our silly "Houries." Follows
Umar-i-Khayyâm, who spiritualized Tasaw-
wof, or Sooffeism, even as the Soofis (Gnos-
tics) spiritualized Moslem Puritanism. The
verses alluded to are:—

You know, my friends, with what a brave carouse
I made a second marriage in my house,
Divorced old barren Reason from my bed
And took the Daughter of the Vine to spouse.
(St. 60, Mr. Fitzgerald's translation.)

[103]

Here "Wine" is used in its mystic sense of entranced Love for the Soul of Souls. Umar was hated and feared because he spoke boldly when his brethren the Soofis dealt in innuendoes. A third quotation has been trained into a likeness of the "Hymn of Life," despite the commonplace and the *navrante vulgarité* which characterize the pseudo-Schiller-Anglo-American School. The same has been done to the words of Isâ (Jesus); for the author, who is well-read in the Ingîl (Evangel), evidently intended the allusion. Mansur el-Hallâj the (Cotton-Cleaner) was stoned for crudely uttering the Pantheistic dogma *Ana 'l Hakk* (I am the Truth, *i.e.*, God), *wa laysa fi-jubbati il' Allah* (and within my coat is nought but God). His blood traced on the ground the first-quoted sentence. Lastly, there is a quotation from "Sardanapalus, son of Anacyndaraxes," etc. : here παῖζε may mean sport; but the context determines the kind of sport intended. The Zâhid is the literal believer in the letter of the Law, opposed to the Soofi, who believes in its spirit: hence the former is called a Zâhiri (outsider), and the latter a Bâtini, an insider. Moses is quoted because he ignored future re-

wards and punishments. As regards the "two
Eternities," Persian and Arab metaphysicians
split Eternity, *i.e.*, the negation of Time, into
two halves, *Azal* (beginninglessness) and *Abad*
(endlessness); both being mere words, gather-
ings of letters with a subjective significance.
In English we use "Eternal" (*Æviternus*,
age-long, life-long) as loosely, by applying it
to three distinct ideas; (1) the habitual, in
popular parlance; (2) the exempt from duration; and (3) the everlasting, which embraces
all duration. "Omniscience-Maker" is the
old Roman sceptic's *Homo fecit Deos*.

The next section is one long wail over the
contradictions, the mysteries, the dark end,
the infinite sorrowfulness of all existence, and
the arcanum of grief which, Luther said, un-
derlies all life. As with Euripides "to live is to
die, to die is to live." Hâjî Abdû borrows the
Hindu idea of the human body. "It is a man-
sion," says Menu, "with bones for its beams
and rafters; with nerves and tendons for cords;
with muscles and blood for cement; with skin
for its outer covering; filled with no sweet
perfume, but loaded with impurities; a man-
sion infested by age and sorrow; the seat of

malady; harassed with pains; haunted with the quality of darkness (Tama-guna), and incapable of standing." The Pot and Potter began with the ancient Egyptians. " Sitting as a potter at the wheel, Cneph (at Philæ) moulds clay, and gives the spirit of life to the nostrils of Osiris." Hence the Genesitic " breath." Then we meet him in the Vedas, the Being " by whom the fictile vase is formed; the clay out of which it is fabricated." We find him next in Jeremiah's "Arise and go down unto the Potter's house," etc. (xviii. 2), and lastly in Romans (ix. 20), " Hath not the potter power over the clay?" No wonder that the first Hand who moulded the man-mud is a *lieu commun* in Eastern thought. The " waste of agony" is Buddhism, or Schopenhauerism pure and simple, I have moulded "Earth on Earth" upon "Seint Ysidre" 's well-known rhymes (A.D. 1440):—

Erthe out of Erthe is wondirli wrouzt,
Erthe out of Erth hath gete a dignity of nouzt,
Erthe upon Erthe hath sett all his thouzt
How that Erthe upon Erthe may be his brouzt, etc.

The " Camel-rider," suggests Ossian, " yet a few years and the blast of the desert comes."

[106]

The dromedary was chosen as Death's vehicle by the Arabs, probably because it bears the Bedouin's corpse to the distant burial-ground, where he will lie among his kith and kin. The end of this section reminds us of: —

> How poor, how rich; how abject, how august,
> How complicate, how wonderful is Man!

The Hâjî now passes to the results of his long and anxious thoughts: I have purposely twisted his exordium into an echo of Milton: —

> Till old experience doth attain
> To something of prophetic strain.

He boldly declares that there is no God as man has created his Creator. Here he is at one with modern thought: — "En général les croyants font le Dieu comme ils sont eux-mêmes," (says J. J. Rousseau, "Confessions," I. 6): "les bons le font bon: les méchants le font méchant: les dévots haineux et bilieux, ne voient que l'enfer, parce qu'ils voudraient damner tout le monde; les âmes aimantes et douces n'y croient guère; et l'un des étonne-ments dont je ne reviens pas est de voir le bon Fénélon en parler dans son Télémaque comme

s'il y croyoit tout de bon: mais j'espère qu'il
mentoit alors; car enfin quelque véridique
qu'on soit, il faut bien mentir quelquefois
quand on est évêque." "Man depicts himself
in his gods," says Schiller. Hence the *Natur-
gott*, the deity of all ancient peoples, and with
which every system began, allowed and ap-
proved of actions distinctly immoral, often
diabolical. Belief became moralized only when
the conscience of the community, and with it
of the individual items, began aspiring to its
golden age, — Perfection. "Dieu est le super-
latif, dont le positif est l'homme," says Carl
Vogt; meaning, that the popular idea of a *nu-
men* is that of a magnified and non-natural man.

He then quotes his authorities. Buddha,
whom the Catholic Church converted to Saint
Josaphat, refused to recognize Ishwara (the
deity), on account of the mystery of the "cruelty of things." Schopenhauer, Miss Cobbe's
model pessimist, who at the humblest distance
represents Buddha in the world of Western
thought, found the vision of man's unhappi-
ness, irrespective of his actions, so overpower-
ing that he concluded the Supreme Will to be
malevolent, "heartless, cowardly, and arro-

gant." Confucius, the "Throneless king, more powerful than all kings," denied a personal deity. The Epicurean idea rules the China of the present day. "God is great, but he lives too far off," say the Turanian Santâls in Aryan India; and this is the general language of man in the Turanian East.

Hâjî Abdû evidently holds that idolatry begins with a personal deity. And let us note that the latter is deliberately denied by the "Thirty-nine Articles." With them God is "a Being without Parts (personality) or Passions." He professes a vague Agnosticism, and attributes popular faith to the fact that Timor fecit Deos; "every religion being, without exception, the child of fear and ignorance" (Carl Vogt). He now speaks as the "Drawer of the Wine," the "Ancient Taverner," the "Old Magus," the "Patron of the Mughân or Magians"; all titles applied to the Soofi as opposed to the Zâhid. His "idols" are the *eidola* (illusions) of Bacon, "having their foundations in the very constitution of man," and therefore appropriately called *fabulæ*. That "Nature's Common Course" is subject to various interpretation, may be easily proved. Aristotle was as

great a subverter as Alexander; but the quasi-
prophetical Stagyrite of the Dark Ages, who
ruled the world till the end of the thirteenth
century, became the "twice execrable" of
Martin Luther; and was finally abolished by
Galileo and Newton. Here I have excised two
stanzas. The first is:—

Theories for truths, fable for fact; system for science
vex the thought
Life's one great lesson you despise — to know that all
we know is nought.

This is in fact:—

Well didst thou say, Athena's noblest son,
The most we know is nothing can be known.

The next is:—

Essence and substance, sequence, cause, beginning,
ending, space and time,
These be the toys of manhood's mind, at once ridicu-
lous and sublime.

He is not the only one who so regards
"bothering Time and Space." A late defini-
tion of the "infinitely great," viz., that the idea
arises from denying form to any figure; of the
"infinitely small," from refusing magnitude to
any figure, is a fair specimen of the "dismal
science"—metaphysics.

NOTES

Another omitted stanza reads:—

How canst thou, Phenomen ! pretend the Noumenon to
mete and span?
Say which were easier probed and proved, Absolute
Being or mortal man?

One would think that he had read Kant on
the "Knowable and the Unknowable," or had
heard of the Yankee lady, who could "differ-
entiate between the Finite and the Infinite."
It is a common-place of the age, in the West
as well as the East, that Science is confined to
phenomena, and cannot reach the Noumena,
the things themselves. This is the scholastic
realism, the "residuum of a bad metaphysic,"
which deforms the system of Comte. With all
its pretensions, it simply means that there are,
or can be conceived, things in themselves (*i.e.*,
unrelated to thought); that we know them to
exist; and, at the same time, that we cannot
know what they are. But who dares say "cannot"? Who can measure man's work when he
shall be as superior to our present selves as we
are to the Cave-man of past time?

The "Chain of Universe" alludes to the
Jain idea that the whole, consisting of intellectual as well as of natural principles, existed

[111]

from all eternity; and that it has been subject
to endless revolutions, whose causes are the
inherent powers of nature, intellectual as well
as physical, without the intervention of a deity.
But the Poet ridicules the "non-human," *i.e.*,
the not-ourselves, the negation of ourselves
and consequently a non-existence. Most Easterns confuse the contradictories, in which one
term stands for something, and the other for
nothing (*e.g.*, ourselves and not-ourselves),
with the contraries (*e.g.*, rich and not-rich =
poor), in which both terms express a something. So the positive-negative "infinite" is
not the complement of "finite," but its negation. The Western man derides the process by
making "not-horse" the complementary entity of "horse." The Pilgrim ends with the
favourite Soofi tenet that the five (six?) senses
are the doors of all human knowledge, and that
no form of man, incarnation of the deity,
prophet, apostle or sage, has ever produced an
idea not conceived within his brain by the sole
operation of these vulgar material agents. Evidently he is neither spiritualist nor idealist.

He then proceeds to show that man depicts
himself in his God, and that "God is the racial

expression"; a pedagogue on the Nile, an abstraction in India, and an astrologer in Chaldæa; where Abraham, says Berosus (Josephus, Ant. I. 7, §2, and II. 9, §2) was "skilful in the celestial science." He notices the Akârana-Zamân (endless Time) of the Guebres, and the working dual, Hormuzd and Ahriman. He brands the God of the Hebrews with pugnacity and cruelty. He has heard of the beautiful creations of Greek fancy which, not attributing a moral nature to the deity, included Theology in Physics; and which, like Professor Tyndall, seemed to consider all matter everywhere alive. We have adopted a very different Unitarianism; Theology, with its one Creator; Pantheism with its "one Spirit's plastic stress"; and Science with its one Energy. He is hard upon Christianity and its "trinal God": I have not softened his expression (لغز = a riddle), although it may offend readers. There is nothing more enigmatical to the Moslem mind than Christian Trinitarianism: all other objections they can get over, not this. Nor is he any lover of Islamism, which, like Christianity, has its ascetic Hebraism and its Hellenic hedonism; with the world of thought moving between these two extremes. The former, defined as predominant or exclusive care for the practice of right, is represented by Semitic and Arab influence, Korânic and Hadîsic. The latter, the religion of humanity, a passion for life and light, for culture and intelligence; for art, poetry and science, is represented in Islamism by the fondly and impiously-cherished memory of the old Guebre kings and heroes, beauties, bards and sages. Hence the mention of Zâl and his son Rostam; of Cyrus and of the Jâm-i-Jamshîd, which may be translated either grail (cup) or mirror: it showed the whole world within its rim; and hence it was called Jâm-i-Jehân-numâ (universe-exposing). The contemptuous expressions about the diet of camel's milk and the meat of the Susmâr, or green lizard, are evidently quoted from Firdausi's famous lines beginning:—

Arab-râ be-jâî rasîd'est kâr.

The Hâjî is severe upon those who make of the Deity a Khwân-i-yaghmâ (or tray of plunder) as the Persians phrase it. He looks upon the shepherds as men,

—Who rob the sheep themselves to clothe.

[114]

NOTES

So Schopenhauer (Leben, etc., by Wilhelm Gewinner) furiously shows how the "English nation ought to treat that set of hypocrites, imposters and money-graspers, the clergy, that annually devours £3,500,000."

The Hâjî broadly asserts that there is no Good and no Evil in the absolute sense as man has made them. Here he is one with Pope:—

And spite of pride, in erring nature's spite
One truth is clear—whatever is, is right.

Unfortunately the converse is just as true:— whatever is, is wrong. Khizr is the Elijah who puzzled Milman. He represents the Soofi, the Bâtini, while Musâ (Moses) is the Zâhid, the Zâhiri; and the strange adventures of the twain, invented by the Jews, have been appropriated by the Moslems. He derides the Freewill of man; and, like Diderot, he detects "pantaloon in a prelate, a satyr in a president, a pig in a priest, an ostrich in a minister, and a goose in a chief clerk." He holds to Fortune, the Τύχη of Alcman, which is, Εὐνομίας τε καὶ Πειθοῦς ἀδελφὰ καὶ Προμαθείας θυγάτηρ, — Chance, the sister of Order and Trust, and the daughter of Forethought. The Scandinavian Spinners of Fate were Urd (the Was, the Past),

Verdandi (the Becoming, or Present), and
Skuld (the To-be, or Future). He alludes to
Plato, who made the Demiourgos create the
worlds by the Logos (the Hebrew Dabar) or
Creative Word, through the Æons. These
Αἰῶνες of the Mystics were spiritual emana-
tions from Αἰών, lit. a wave of influx, an age,
period, or day; hence the Latin *ævum*, and the
Welsh Awen, the stream of inspiration falling
upon a bard. Basilides, the Egypto-Christian,
made the Creator evolve seven Æons or Ptero-
mata (fulnesses); from two of whom, Wisdom
and Power, proceeded the 365 degrees of
Angels. All were subject to a Prince of
Heaven, called Abraxas, who was himself
under guidance of the chief Æon, Wisdom.
Others represent the first Cause to have produced an Æon or Pure Intelligence; the first
a second, and so forth till the tenth. This was
material enough to affect Hyle, which thereby
assumed a spiritual form. Thus the two incom-
patibles combined in the Scheme of Creation.

He denies the three ages of the Buddhists:
the wholly happy; the happy; mixed with misery, and the miserable tinged with happiness,
—the present. The Zoroastrians had four,

each of 3,000 years. In the first, Hormuzd, the good-god, ruled alone; then Ahriman, the bad-god, began to rule subserviently: in the third both ruled equally; and in the last, now current, Ahriman has gained the day.

Against the popular idea that man has caused the misery of this world, he cites the ages, when the Old Red Sandstone bred gigantic cannibal fishes; when the Oolites produced the mighty reptile tyrants of air, earth, and sea; and when the monsters of the Eocene and Miocene periods shook the ground with their ponderous tread. And the world of waters is still a hideous scene of cruelty, carnage, and destruction.

He declares Conscience to be a geographical and chronological accident. Thus he answers the modern philosopher whose soul was overwhelmed by the marvel and the awe of two things, "the starry heaven above and the moral law within." He makes the latter sense a development of the gregarious and social instincts; and so travellers have observed that the moral is the last step in mental progress. His Moors are the savage Dankali and other negroid tribes, who offer a cup of milk with

one hand and stab with the other. He trans-
lates literally the Indian word Hâthî (an elephant), the animal with the Hâth (hand, or
trunk). Finally he alludes to the age of active
volcanoes, the present, which is merely tem-
porary, the shifting of the Pole, and the spec-
tacle to be seen from Mushtari, or the planet
Jupiter.

The Hâjî again asks the old, old question,
What is Truth? And he answers himself, after
the fashion of the wise Emperor of China,
"Truth hath not an unchanging name." A
modern English writer says: "I have long been
convinced by the experience of my life, as a
pioneer of various heterodoxies, which are
rapidly becoming orthodoxies, that nearly
all truth is temperamental to us, or given in
the affections and intuitions; and that dis-
cussion and inquiry do little more than feed
temperament." Our poet seems to mean that
the Perceptions, when they perceive truly,
convey objective truth, which is universal;
whereas the Reflectives and the Sentiments,
the working of the moral region, or the middle lobe of the phrenologists, supplies only
subjective truth, personal and individual. Thus

[118]

to one man the axiom, *Opes irritamenta malo-rum*, represents a distinct fact; while another holds wealth to be an incentive for good. Evidently both are right, according to their lights.

Hâjî Abdû cites Plato and Aristotle, as usual with Eastern songsters, who delight in Mantik (logic). Here he appears to mean that a false proposition is as real a proposition as one that is true. "Faith moves mountains" and "Manet immota fides" are evidently quotations. He derides the teaching of the "First Council of the Vatican" (cap. v.), "all the faithful are little children listening to the voice of Saint Peter," who is the "Prince of the Apostles." He glances at the fancy of certain modern physicists, "devotion is a definite molecular change in the convolution of grey pulp." He notices with contumely the riddle of which Milton speaks so glibly, where the Dialoguists,

— reasoned high
Of providence, foreknowledge, will and fate,
Fixed fate, free will, foreknowledge absolute.

In opposition to the orthodox Mohammedan tenets which make Man's soul his percipient Ego, an entity, a unity, the Soofi considers it a fancy, opposed to body, which is a fact; at most a state of things, not a thing; a consensus of faculties whereof our frames are but the phenomena. This is not contrary to Genesitic legend. The Hebrew Ruach and Arabic Ruh, now perverted to mean soul or spirit, simply signify wind or breath, the outward and visible sign of life. Their later schools are even more explicit: " For that which befalls man befalls beasts; as the one dies, so does the other; they have all one death; all go unto one place " (Eccles. iii 19). But the modern soul, a nothing, a string of negations, a negative in chief, is thus described in the Mahâbhârat: "It is indivisible, inconceivable, inconceptible: it is eternal, universal, permanent, immovable: it is invisible and unalterable." Hence the modern spiritualism which, rejecting materialism, can use only material language.

These, says the Hâjî, are mere sounds. He would not assert "Verba gignunt verba," but "Verba gignunt res,"a step further. The idea is Bacon's "idola fori, omnium molestissima," the twofold illusions of language; either the names of things that have no existence in fact, or the names of things whose idea is confused and ill-defined.

He derives the Soul-idea from the "savage ghost" which Dr. Johnson defined to be a "kind of shadowy being." He justly remarks that it arose (perhaps) in Egypt; and was not invented by the "People of the Book." By this term Moslems denote Jews and Christians who have a recognized revelation, while their ignorance refuses it to Guebres, Hindus, and Confucians.

He evidently holds to the doctrine of progress. With him protoplasm is the Yliastron, the Prima Materies. Our word matter is derived from the Sanskrit मात्रा (mâtrâ), which, however, signifies properly the invisible type of visible matter; in modern language, the substance distinct from the sum of its physical and chemical properties. Thus, Mâtrâ exists only in thought, and is not recognizable by the action of the five senses. His "Chain of Being" reminds us of Prof. Huxley's Pedigree of the Horse, Orohippus, Mesohippus, Meiohippus, Protohippus, Pleiohippus, and Equus. He has evidently heard of modern biology, or Hylozoism, which holds its quarter-million

species of living beings, animal and vegetable,
to be progressive modifications of one great
fundamental unity, an unity of so-called" mental faculties" as well as of bodily structure.
And this is the jelly-speck. He scoffs at the
popular idea that man is the great central figure round which all things gyrate like mari-
onettes; in fact, the anthropocentric era of
Draper, which, strange to say, lives by the side
of the telescope and the microscope. As man
is of recent origin, and may end at an early
epoch of the macrocosm, so before his birth
all things revolved round nothing, and may
continue to do so after his death.

The Hâjî, who elsewhere denounces "compound ignorance," holds that all evil comes
from error; and that all knowledge has been
developed by overthrowing error, the ordi-
nary channel of human thought. He ends this
section with a great truth. There are things
which human Reason or Instinct matured, in
its undeveloped state, cannot master; but Reason is a Law to itself. Therefore we are not
bound to believe, or to attempt belief in, any
thing which is contrary or contradictory to
Reason. Here he is diametrically opposed to

Rome, who says, "Do not appeal to History; that is private judgment. Do not appeal to Holy Writ; that is heresy. Do not appeal to Reason; that is Rationalism."

He holds with the Patriarchs of Hebrew Holy Writ, that the present life is all-sufficient for an intellectual (not a sentimental) being; and, therefore, that there is no want of a Heaven or a Hell. With far more contradiction the Western poet sings:—

> Hell hath no limits, nor is circumscribed
> In one self-place; but when we are in hell,
> And where hell is there must we ever be,
> And, to be short, when all this world dissolves,
> And every creature shall be purified,
> All places shall be hell which are not heaven.

For what want is there of a Hell when all are pure? He enlarges upon the ancient Buddhist theory, that Happiness and Misery are equally distributed among men and beasts; some enjoy much and suffer much; others the reverse. Hence Diderot declares, "Sober passions produce only the commonplace . . . the man of moderate passion lives and dies like a brute." And again we have the half truth:—

> That the mark of rank in nature
> Is capacity for pain.

The latter implies an equal capacity for pleasure, and thus the balance is kept.

Hâjî Abdû then proceeds to show that Faith is an accident of birth. One of his omitted distichs says : —

> Race makes religion ; true ! but aye upon the Maker acts the made,
> A finite God, and infinite sin, in lieu of raising man, degrade.

In a manner of dialogue he introduces the various races each fighting to establish its own belief. The Frank (Christian) abuses the Hindu, who retorts that he is of Mlenchha, mixed or impure, blood, a term applied to all non-Hindus. The same is done by Nazarene and Mohammedan; by the Confucian, who believes in nothing, and by the Soofi, who naturally has the last word. The association of the Virgin Mary and St. Joseph with the Trinity, in the Roman and Greek Churches, makes many Moslems conclude that Christians believe not in three but in five Persons. So an Englishman writes of the early Fathers, "They not only said that $3 = 1$, and that $1 = 3$: they professed to explain how that curious arithmetical combination had been brought about. The Indivisible had been divided, and yet was not divided: it was divisible, and yet it was indivisible; black was white and white was black; and yet there were not two colours but one colour; and whoever did not believe it would be damned." The Arab quotation runs in the original:—

Ahsanu 'l-Makâni l' il-Fatâ 'l-Jehannamu

The best of places for (the generous) youth is Gehenna.

Gehenna, alias Jahim, being the fiery place of eternal punishment. And the second saying, *Al- nâr wa lâ 'l-' Ar*—"Fire (of Hell) rather than Shame,"—is equally condemned by the Koranist. The Gustâkhi (insolence) of Fate is the expression of Umar-i-Khayyam (St. xxx):—

What, without asking hither hurried *whence?*
And, without asking *whither* hurried hence!
  Oh many a cup of this forbidden wine
Must drown the memory of that insolence.

Soofistically, the word means "the coquetry of the beloved one," the divinæ particula auræ. And the section ends with Pope's:—

He can't be wrong whose life is in the right.

CONCLUSION

H ERE the Hâjî ends his practical study of mankind. The image of Destiny playing with men as pieces is a view common amongst Easterns. His idea of wisdom is once more Pope's:—

And all our knowledge is ourselves to know.

(Essay IV. 398.)

Regret, *i.e.*, repentance, was one of the forty-two deadly sins of the Ancient Egyptians. "Thou shalt not consume thy heart," says the Ritual of the Dead, the negative justification of the soul or ghost (Lepsius "Alteste des Todtenbuchs"). We have borrowed competitive examination from the Chinese; and, in these morbid days of weak introspection and retrospection, we might learn wisdom from the sturdy old Khemites. When he sings "Abjure the Why and seek the How," he refers to the old Scholastic difference of the

[126]

Demonstratio propter quid (why is a thing?), as opposed to *Demonstratio quia* (*i.e.* that a thing is). The "great Man" shall end with becoming deathless, as Shakespeare says in his noble sonnet:—

And Death once dead, there's no more dying then!

Like the great Pagans, the Hâjî holds that man was born good, while the Christian, "tormented by the things divine," cleaves to the comforting doctrine of innate sinfulness. Hence the universal tenet, that man should do good in order to gain by it here or hereafter; the "enlightened selfishness," that says, Act well and get compound interest in a future state. The allusion to the "Theist-word" apparently means that the votaries of a personal Deity must believe in the absolute foreknowledge of the Omniscient in particulars as in generals. The Rule of Law emancipates man; and its exceptions are the gaps left by his ignorance. The wail over the fallen flower, etc., reminds us of the Pulambal (Lamentations) of the Anti-Brahminical writer, "Pathira-Giri yâr." The allusion to Mâyâ is from Dâs Kabîr:—

[127]

Mâyâ mare, na man mare, mar mar gayâ sarîr.

Illusion dies, the mind dies not though dead and
gone the flesh.

Nirwâna, I have said, is partial extinction by
being merged in the Supreme, not to be con-
founded with Pari-nirwâna or absolute annihilation. In the former also, dying gives
birth to a new being, the embodiment of
karma (deeds), good and evil, done in the
countless ages of transmigration.

Here ends my share of the work. On the
whole it has been considerable. I have omitted,
as has been seen, sundry stanzas, and I have
changed the order of others. The text has
nowhere been translated verbatim; in fact, a
familiar European turn has been given to
many sentiments which were judged too Oriental. As the metre adopted by Hâjî Abdû
was the *Bahr Tawîl* (long verse), I thought
it advisable to preserve that peculiarity, and to
fringe it with the rough, unobtrusive rhyme
of the original.

Vive, valeque!

REFLECTIONS

This selection of Idries Shah's own fables, aphorisms and teachings is now in its third edition and continues to be extremely popular.

Pocket-sized, it is immensely entertaining and at the same time offers an alternative view of our society that is both refreshing and profitable.

'More wisdom than I have found in any other books this year'

Pat Williams *Review of the Year*, BBC

'It seems to oblige the mind to scorn the satisfaction of going from A to B in favour of an approach from a different angle, taking in unsuspected territory, hatches out as modified behaviour.'

The Evening News

REFLECTIONS
by Idries Shah
The Octagon Press Ltd., 75p net.

THE SECRET GARDEN OF
MAHMUD SHABISTARI

This book, by an almost unknown Persian sage of the thirteenth century, is among the greatest classics of spirituality of the East.

Though written over six hundred years ago, as a reviewer correctly pointed out, 'Shabistari's ideas can usefully be applied to our own contemporary social problems.'

John A. Subhan says of it:—

'his work is important out of all comparison . . . because it is a compendium of Sufi terminology in the form of question and answer.'

THE SECRET GARDEN of Mahmud Shabistari,
Translated by Johnson Pasha from the Aga Khan version.
Octagon Press Ltd., £1.50 net.

SPECIAL PROBLEMS IN THE STUDY
OF SUFI IDEAS

This important monograph constitutes the whole text of Idries Shah's Seminar at Sussex University, fully annotated, indexed and with a bibliography and notes.

It knits together the available knowledge about Sufi thought and literature in its passage through many deforming influences, such as the development of cults, the mis-interpretation by literalist scholars, and the fallacious comparisons of committed 'specialists.'

'Masterful essay . . . he has ably presented Sufism to the West and has conveyed its deep sense of reality to modern man . . .'

Professor A. Reza Arasteh,
Psychology of the Sufi Way, 1972.

SPECIAL PROBLEMS IN THE STUDY OF SUFI IDEAS
by Idries Shah
The Octagon Press Ltd., 40p.

TEACHINGS OF RUMI

THE MASNAWI

Jalaluddin Rumi's great work, *The Masnavi,* was 43 years in the writing. During the past seven hundred years, this book, called by the Iranians 'The Koran in Persian,' a tribute paid to no other book, has occupied a central place in Sufism.

'*The Masnavi* is full of profound mysteries, and a most important book in the study of Sufism — mysteries which must, for the most part, be left to the discernment of the reader.'

F. Hadland Davis

'To the Sufi, if not to anyone else, this book speaks from a different dimension, yet a dimension which is in a way within his deepest self.'

Idries Shah

'The greatest mystical poet of any age.'

Professor R. A. Nicolson

'It can well be argued that he is the supreme mystical poet of all mankind.'

Professor A. J. Arberry

TEACHINGS OF RUMI The Masnavi:
Abridged and translated by E. H. Whinfield.
Octagon Press Ltd.,
£4.00 net (hardback) £3.00 net (softback)

CARAVAN OF DREAMS

Teaching stories of the dervish philosophers and mystics, writings by Idries Shah on Mecca and on Islam, poetry, proverbs, allegories, and symbolic tales of amazing richness and variety. The collection as a whole makes delightful reading, and at the same time brings the reader closer to the spiritual essence of the Middle East.

'Real possibilities and practical alternatives to our present ways of operation . . . known and tested activity; relevant, fruitful and urgent for our present society'

New Society

'Like the marvellous dream landscapes you entered with fairy-tales as a child.'

Doris Lessing, *The Listener*

CARAVAN OF DREAMS
by Idries Shah
The Octagon Press Ltd., £1.75 net.

THE SPIRIT OF THE EAST

Today the kinship of all religious thought and dogma is becoming more apparent to mankind — and the value of Oriental thought to the Occidental mind is obvious. Here is a selection from Moslem, Parsee, Hindu, Hebrew, Confucian and other sources, chosen not only for their spiritual worth but also for the particular virtues of each creed which they represent.

The aim of this book is to introduce readers to the religious thought of the East, which — for reasons of language and other difficulties — they might otherwise have considered inaccessible.

THE SPIRIT OF THE EAST
Sirdar Ikbal Ali Shah
The Octagon Press Ltd.,
£3.50 net. (hardback) £1.75 net. (paperback)

FOLK TALES OF CENTRAL ASIA

A collection of stories selected entirely from the oral tradition: from servants and royal courts, from teahouses and caravanserais — some of them just ahead of the industrial development which helps to wipe out such delightful examples of the treasures of human culture.

Amina Shah, who was brought up both in the East and West, has written and broadcast extensively on Eastern traditional lore.

FOLK TALES OF CENTRAL ASIA
by Amina Shah
The Octagon Press Ltd., £1.50 net.